A Ladybird Bible Book

Paul the Traveller

Text by Jenny Robertson

Illustrations by Alan Parry

Scripture Union/Ladybird

'We must hide!' whispered Paul. An angry crowd was marching up the street looking for the men who were teaching about Jesus and upsetting the old religions. Paul and his friends Silas and Timothy slipped away. The crowd hammered on doors, looking for them. They found a man called Jason, in whose house Paul had been staying. At once they dragged him off to the rulers of the town. 'This man's an enemy of the Roman Emperor!' they yelled. 'He follows another King, called Jesus!' The rulers were furious. Jason had no chance to explain. He had to pay a large fine before they would let him go.

As soon as he was released he went to find Paul and his friends and helped them escape from the town.

Paul, Silas and Timothy made their way quickly to another city, Berea. The people there were friendly, and listened eagerly to their teaching about Jesus. But danger still followed Paul. His enemies came after him and tried to turn the people of Berea against him. So, while Silas and Timothy stayed to help the new believers, Paul set out to dodge his enemies. He

headed for the coast, but then, instead of boarding a ship, he travelled on to Athens, the most famous of all the Greek cities.

While Paul waited for Silas and Timothy to join him there, he spent his time looking round the city. When he noticed the hundreds of statues of different gods and goddesses which the people worshipped, Paul wanted to tell them about the true God.

The Athenians enjoyed discussing ideas of all kinds, so they were interested to hear Paul. They asked him to come and talk to their city council. Paul went gladly. He told them about Jesus who had come to die so that their wrong-doings could be forgiven. He told them how God had raised Jesus from the dead. Some people believed Paul, but many of them laughed at him. They thought he was talking nonsense. 'Who is this idiot?' they asked. But Paul didn't mind. He knew that following Jesus was more important than being thought clever.

Paul soon moved on to the busy port of Corinth, just north of Athens. Here he made friends with a Jew called Aquila and his wife Priscilla. Aquila was a tent maker, and, as Paul had learned the same trade, he stayed with them and helped them with their work. Together they sat and stitched the heavy tents. By now Silas and Timothy had rejoined Paul. They went all over Corinth, teaching the people about Jesus. They stayed there for a year and a half, talking to anyone who would listen, and helping the new believers follow Jesus in a city where most people worshipped other gods.

Finally Paul left Corinth and made his way back to Jerusalem where the leaders of the Christians lived. He had plenty of exciting news for them! Then he went on to visit his old friends in the towns where he had first taught people about Jesus.

At last he made his way to Ephesus, a large sea port, with a splendid temple to the goddess, Diana. Some of the people there had already become Christians, but most of them worshipped the Roman gods, and many practised

magic. They had heavy books of spells, and little scrolls with charms written on them, which they used to carry with them to bring them luck. When Paul arrived he began to teach the people about Jesus. He also healed many sick people in the name of Jesus, and drove away evil spirits. Soon the people realised that Jesus was more powerful than any magic. Some of the Christians, who had practised magic, realised that what they had been doing was wrong. They decided to have nothing more to do with it. Solemnly they brought their books and scrolls to the market place and made a huge bonfire. Thousands of valuable books were burnt up. News of this soon spread, and more people came to believe in Jesus because of it.

There were many silversmiths in Ephesus who earned money by making models of the goddess Diana and her temple. After Paul had been there three years they grew worried. 'If things go on like this,' they grumbled, 'there'll be nobody praying to Diana any more. They'll all be following Jesus, and we'll be out of a job!'

When the townspeople heard this they were furious and they began to shout, 'Long live Diana! Long live Diana!' They found two of Paul's friends and dragged them off to the theatre where the public meetings were held. For two hours the people chanted and shouted. Nobody could calm them down. At last the town clerk managed to make himself heard: 'We all know that our goddess, Diana, is great and powerful. Nobody disputes that. But you have brought these men here although they have done nothing that is criminal. If you have any complaints make them in the law courts. Don't get Ephesus a bad name by causing a riot!' The crowd listened to the town clerk and went home without making any more trouble. But Paul knew it was no longer safe for him to stay there.

So Paul left Ephesus and travelled on to visit more of the Christian churches which he had helped to start on his first journeys.

After several months, Paul decided to go back to Jerusalem. On the way he and his friends stopped at the port of Troas. They stayed with the Christians who lived there, and on their last evening they all met together to worship God. The meeting was held in a room at the top of a tall building, and it was crowded. People sat close together on the floor or perched on the window sills. Smoky oil lamps hung from the

ceiling, and the air was stuffy and warm. Paul began to talk – he had so much to say before he left! One of the boys, called Eutychus, who was sitting on the window sill, began to doze. His head slipped back, and before anyone could help him he slid backwards through the window, and crashed to the ground. His friends rushed downstairs, but he was dead. 'Don't worry!' Paul put his arms round Eutychus. 'Look! He's alive!' Sure enough, Eutychus opened his eyes and then got to his feet. Overjoyed, his friends helped him upstairs again, and there they stayed until morning, praising God, and listening to Paul's message.

The journey back to Jerusalem took Paul near Ephesus again, but he did not want to lose time by stopping there. Instead he sent a message to the leaders of the church asking them to meet him at the port where his boat was docked. When they arrived he spoke solemnly to them. 'I don't know what will happen to me in Jerusalem. God has warned me to expect trouble and imprisonment wherever I go, but that doesn't worry me! All I want is to finish the work the Lord Jesus gave me to do: telling everyone I can the good news about him. So please pray for me; and keep on following Jesus yourselves.' Then Paul and the leaders knelt and prayed together. Sadly they said goodbye. They knew they would never see Paul again.

At last Paul reached Jerusalem. The Christians there welcomed him warmly, but they were worried, for they knew Paul had many enemies there. And it was not long before they attacked him. Some of them saw Paul in the streets with a friend from Ephesus. When they next saw Paul he was in the Temple where only Jewish men were allowed to be. At once they decided he had brought his Ephesian friend with him. 'Kill him!' they yelled. 'He's brought non-Jews into our most holy place! He's defying our sacred

laws!' At once a crowd gathered and dragged Paul out of the Temple. They hit and kicked him, shouting angrily as they did so. Then someone told the commander of the Roman soldiers in Jerusalem that there was a riot. Quickly he took some men and marched to the Temple. He stopped the crowd beating Paul and had him arrested. The soldiers had to hoist him up on their shoulders and carry him away to keep the crowd from tearing him apart. Paul tried to explain to the crowd about Jesus, but they wouldn't listen.

The Roman commander could not under-
stand what Paul had done to enrage the crowd.
He ordered his men to beat him until he told
them. So the soldiers stripped Paul and tied him
to a post. Then Paul calmly told them that he
was a Roman citizen. They were breaking the
law even by tying him up without giving him a
fair trial first! Anxiously the commander ques-
tioned Paul. 'I had to buy my citizenship,' said
the commander. 'It cost me a lot of money.'

'I was born a Roman citizen!' Paul replied
quietly. Frightened, the commander had Paul's
chains taken off him.

'Paul thinks he's safe now he's with the Romans, but we'll get him yet!' muttered his enemies. They vowed not to eat or drink until they had killed him. 'We'll ask the chief priests to get the Romans to send Paul to them for further questioning, and we'll kill him on his way there,' they plotted. They didn't see the

little boy who crouched in the shadows and heard every word. He was Paul's nephew! Quietly he slipped away to the fort to warn his uncle.

At once Paul called an officer who took the boy to the commander.

The commander led the boy to a quiet corner. 'What do you have to tell me, son?' he asked. When he heard the boy's story he sent him home, telling him not to breathe a word to anyone. Then he ordered two hundred foot soldiers, seventy horsemen and two hundred spearmen to get ready to take Paul out of Jerusalem as soon as it got dark. 'Take him down to Caesarea and let Governor Felix deal with the case!'

The commander wrote a letter to Felix about Paul: 'The Jews were about to kill this man, but I found out he was a Roman citizen, so I stepped in to save his life. He seems to have broken some Jewish law. I can't find him guilty of any crime against Rome. The Jews are still plotting against him, so I am sending him to you.'

It wasn't quite the truth, but it would never do for Governor Felix to find out that he had put a Roman citizen in chains and nearly had him beaten!

Paul left Jerusalem safely, surrounded by armed men. He knew God was looking after him. The night before he had seen Jesus in a dream, standing beside him. 'Don't be afraid,' Jesus had encouraged him. 'You have told people about me here in Jerusalem – now I want you to go and do the same in Rome.'

And so Paul felt glad as he rode along. His greatest wish had always been to speak for Jesus in Rome, the great city where the Emperor ruled. Now, perhaps through all this trouble, his wish would be fulfilled!

The next day they arrived at Caesarea, and Paul was taken before the governor. Felix read the letter from the commander in Jerusalem, but he decided to do nothing until Paul's enemies arrived from Jerusalem to tell their side of the story. Felix was a poor governor and a cruel man. In the end he simply left Paul in prison, hoping that he would give him a bribe to get out. Paul spent two years under guard, but he was certain that one day, either as a free man or a prisoner, he would set off on his travels again to speak about Jesus in Rome.

Travelling was difficult and dangerous in Paul's time. Paul wrote a letter to some Christians in Corinth and described the dangers he had to face on his journeys – 'I have been in three shipwrecks, and once I spent twenty-four hours in the water. In my many travels I have been in danger from floods and from robbers, in danger from fellow-Jews and from Gentiles; there have been dangers in the cities, dangers in the wilds, dangers on the high seas, and dangers from false friends.' – Not everybody had the same trouble as Paul, but journeys were difficult enough.

Means of Transport

Animals

Most travelling was done on foot. When people did ride they used donkeys which were sure-footed and strong. Camels were used for journeys across the desert, and horses were used by wealthier people to pull chariots, but neither were as popular as the donkey.

Vehicles

Heavy carts drawn by oxen were used on farms. Different chariots, large and small, drawn by horses were used for some journeys where the roads were good enough.

Roads

The Romans built good roads, easy to travel on, and kept in good repair. However, these roads were not built everywhere, and many places were linked only by earth roads which were dusty in the summer, and muddy in the winter rains. It was along these roads that robbers lurked.